Hearts Crossing

Poems

by

Nely Sanchez

Hearts Crossing
Poems

Second Edition

Copyright © 2012 - 2022 by Nely Sanchez

All Rights Reserved

All poems in this book are original works by the author. No part of this book may be reproduced, scanned or transmitted in any form, or by any means whatsoever (electronic, mechanical or otherwise) without the prior written permission and consent of the publisher, except where permitted by law.

ISBN 13: 978-1-951137-23-6

BCLS Creative Publishing Group

~ To Jaime ~

Thank you

For everything

Table of Contents

Time Comes Around	9
Legacy Unwanted	12
Nightmare	14
Love Knocks	15
His Eyes	16
The Day You Left	17
Jasmine In The Air	18
I Saw Him Then	20
Letters	21
Just The Way I Am	22
Apologies	23
Just Enough	24
Tell Me	26

Light Of Fire	28
A Crystal Full Of Shine	29
Why Can't You Hear Me?	30
He Turned His Back On Me	32
Arms Of Another	33
Black Aura	34
To Deceive	35
Shroud Of Ice	36
I Invite You To The Night	38
Blue Night	40
Deep Waters	45
Don't Feel Sorry For Me	46
Frost On My Windows	47
No Good-Byes	49
Little Bluebird	50

My Lover	51
Luna	53
A Love Like Ours	55
As The Dawn	60
About The Author	63

Hearts Crossing

Poems

Time Comes Around

I went to see her
After years of being away

She sat old and frail
But still with much to say

Condemnation and pain-
Off her tongue
Came the blame

And with all her ability
She took no responsibility
For the damage
That she'd once produced

And with casual simplicity
And cold, raw audacity
The past
She quickly reduced-

To moments of time
The blame to be mine

The once child
So quiet and shy

Words thrown out to shame
Continued to blame
The now woman
Wanting to fly-

To a land far away
A new world
I have made
Surrounded by sunshine and grace

I give my forgiveness
With God as my witness
I turn and walk away
From this place

The old pain and grief
I leave at this door
Knowing full well
I belong here no more

Time comes around
For the many
And the few

To show new horizons
To show life anew

Legacy Unwanted

I see it there-
Out over cold waters

Shades of blue
Shades of pain
Of a childhood lost
Never to return again

The sound of a father's whisper
On those shameful nights

Lies and secrets
Will be brought out to light

Fear and resentment
Sent away on a breeze

To crash into mountainsides
In far away seas

We all answer to someone

If not here-
Then there…

For a legacy of shame
A legacy of despair

You died tonight
No tears were shed

With a shrug of the shoulders
Or a nod of the head-

Your daughters move on
No prayer is said

Nightmare

In my nightmare
Ugly memories
Rake over me
Pulling the breath from my lips

As I reach out in pain
Unable to gain
My grasp on your fingertips

Love Knocks

Love knocks
Gently at your door
Wanting to get in from the cold

But baggage and hurt
Help you keep love at bay
From all of your secrets untold

His Eyes

His eyes
So bright-
Glisten like a jewel
When the light of the sun
Casts its shine on them

How I wish
His eyes would look onto me
With love and desire

But his eyes
His eyes-
They belong to another

The Day You Left

I once loved you
But never before had I cried

As on the day you left me
You left me free to fly

But still I tried in vain to claim you
To retrieve what I thought was mine

But the winds were out against me
Pushing me back behind the line

Jasmine In The Air

Jasmine in the air
On an India scented night
Listen to the sounds
Of pleasure taking flight

Cries for more
Dark hands
On my body roam

Expert movement
On curves and caves
Passion and heat
The night craves

Exotic black eyes
And I the prey
Give in willingly
And no other way

Midnight folds
In waves of darkened blue

A pool of love in eyes
Reflect from you

Desire surrounds me
On this starry night
My man's dark skin
Is my delight

I Saw Him Then

I saw him then-
Tall, with broad shoulders
Thick arms
Kind smile
As he introduced himself to the room

The women blushed
Grateful for his attention
Lingering on a handshake
Peering into his dark eyes
Searching for some connection

And I,
Sipping my wine
In awe myself
Of the man so fine-
And knowing full well
He would become mine

Letters

Letters come
And letters go

Like summer heat
And winter snow

Years go by

First one
Then two

Tell me again-
When will I see you?

Just The Way I Am

You gather my feet in your palms
And play with my painted toes

You caress my not-so-firm thighs
And you kiss my imperfect nose

You enjoy the swell of my belly
You're proud of the stretch marks
On my hips

I feel your eyes adore me
I taste desire on your lips

Oh, my luck from Heaven
That it was always in His plan

That you should come to love me
Love me just the way I am

Apologies

Years went by
Like waves in the ocean
Lies-
Dominated our world

Pain and regret
Too soon to forget
I now live with everyday

Apologies
Never too late to say
I say them to you now

For the hidden sins
I myself
Have committed against you

Just Enough

You gave me,

Just enough, to keep me wanting,
In the early hours of the morning,
Though the night was long
And not a moment was wasted.

You give me,

Just enough, to make me need it,
For your demands,
Swift as a storm,
Keep me humming through the night.

I took,

Just enough, to keep me begging
For a continuance of
Ice and fire,
And rough desire-
At your command.

I gave you,

Just enough, to leave you wanting
To take me over once more,
In my complete submission,
Questioning nothing-

I followed.

Tell Me

Walking happily together
On cool winter mornings
When the sun shines bright
On glittery snow packed deep
Under our feet
With a blinding light

Tell me,
Am I really to be with you?

On a sunny beach
With warm waves
Crashing at our feet
A smile on my face
And you within my reach

Tell me,
Am I really to be with you?

On moonlit evenings
With stars in our eyes
Your arm around my shoulders
And in our hands
A glass of wine

Tell me,
Am I really to be with you?

On frequent nights
That have come my way
An empty bed is where I pray
Wondering if I should leave or stay

I ask myself,
Am I really to be with you?

Light Of Fire

You were lost at the time

Screaming in dark places
Drowning in glue
Obstacles in your path
Tripping you

As waves of unfriendly shadows
Swallowed you whole
The Sun-
Light of Fire
A memory no more

Then she arrived
Friend-
Like an angel
Helped you carry the torch

With the new shining light
You walked homeward bound
Once you were lost
But now you are found

A Crystal Full Of Shine

They misused you
A crystal full of shine
They had you in their hands
A beauty, valuable and fine

And like a precious glass of water
Carelessly spilled onto the floor
They brushed your love aside
Hurting you all the more

Let me hold the glass of water
That gently holds your heart
I would walk through a wall of fire
And never spill a drop

Why Can't You Hear Me?

I spoke to you
But my words fell on empty ears

The problem is there
But you deny

You close your eyes
To your worst fears

Still, the evidence is around you
You see it-
But then you don't

You decide to close your eyes
You pretend everything is all right

You can change it
But you won't

I spoke to you
But my words fell on empty ears
It's harder now to dry my tears

I speak to you
Why can't you hear me?

He Turned His Back On Me

He turned his back on me
With pain in his heart
But with some weight
Off his shoulders
And a sparkle in his eyes

For his new love was
Waiting for him
And the excitement of it all
Meant so much to him that day

But a cloud came over me
When my lover slipped away

Because it was easier
For him to leave me
Than it was
For him to stay

Arms Of Another

Why did you have to leave
To the arms of another?

To her life
To her home

While I stand here
Disbelieving you're gone

I ache with the memories
Of our years in my heart

As I live with a coldness
That with time-
Does not seem to part

Black Aura

What were you thinking
When you walked my way?

Giving me a funny grin
With your arrogant sway

Thinking you knew all about me-
Where I'd been
And where I'd stayed

You,
Sarcastic and evil
I could see a mile away

That the black aura around you
Is with you to stay

To Deceive

To deceive is to have
The face of an angel
And a soul from hell

Coming from you
I could not tell

Until you left me-
Leaving behind a caress
Like an angels touch on my skin

Shroud Of Ice

The frozen night air
Touches my lips
As it comes down upon me, cold

Alone on my bed
No warmth for my head
As the darkness around me folds

In my quiet despair
I move to a chair
Missing my lover's warm touch

His absence is key
To the feelings in me
As the memories that surround me are such-

That I cannot escape
Through the house - nor the gate
The love that he took out from me

As this shroud of ice
That I'm desperate to slice
Surrounds me and won't let me be

I Invite You To The Night

I invite you to the night
If you'll come out with me

We can hide in black shadows
Where no one can see

We can swim in deep waters
Beneath swelling waves

Or swim in the darkness-
Of blue water caves

I invite you to the night
Where no one will see

Behind dark-draped windows,
Waiting-
I'll be

I invite you to the night
But only if you'll come-

Into my arms,
Until the rising of sun

Blue Night

Last night I had a dream
That I stood in my childhood home
And each room glowed
Softly with Christmas lights-

As I moved along toward the front room
Where the Christmas tree stood bright
And the house was warm, but-

The front door was open
To the cold night air, and-

I stepped out and down the stairs
While the glittery snow crunched
Beneath my bare feet

At the sidewalk
All was quiet
On this once noisy street, and

The blue night was fresh as
The crisp snow fell on my hot skin

I looked back at the house
As my mother appeared at the door
Disturbing my silence and peace

She warned it was cold-
That I should put on a coat

She sounded caring and concerned
Not like in real life-

So I waved to that kind woman
Wanting to know her more

But she backed into the house
And away from me

As usual-

I then turned as headlights
Cut through the eerie blue night
And a car parked near

I watched the familiar driver
Walk across
To my side of the street, and-

This man-
This man-

Who was once my neighbor and friend
And that as a child, I had loved-
Called out to me in his soft voice

"Hey, beautiful"-

He called me by his usual
Term of endearment
And his smile cut through my heart

But he waved good-bye to me
Then turned and walked away

Just as I made a move
To run to him-

I, the woman
No longer the young girl, but-

I panicked
As my frozen feet
Could not move

And my voice was no more

And my reaching arms
He could not see
As he hurried fast away from me

Until the blue night wrapped him
In her dark arms, and-

He was gone

Just as the Christmas lights
Turned off
From room to room
In my, now, cold and empty house

And as I stood in the darkness
Of the frozen blue night
Melting in the snow

 I somehow realized
That even in my dreams
I am always alone
And that even in my dreams
I should have known

Deep Waters

I swim through the fog
Of my dreams-

Afraid

Listening to the screams
Of my memories

Pulling me beneath
Deep waters

Don't Feel Sorry For Me

I made a mistake

Gave my heart out to take

My lessons I have learned the hard way-

But you don't need to feel sorry for me

Frost On My Windows

Frost on my windows
On this cold, cold night
Red swollen eyes
From tears I've cried

Heart beating fast
An ache so deep
A teddy bear I cuddle with
Watches me weep

Fatigue and weariness
Does not seem to end
Months gone by
I twist and bend

Chills in my body
The quilts can't outrun
Time is running out
I'm coming undone

Where is my lover?
In the arms of another

I am cold
While she has him
Warm

This must end
I must let him go
If not for his sake
Then for my soul

No Good-Byes

You never say good-bye, Blue Eyes,
When our talk is through.

You simply smile
And turn around
And walk away, it's true.

So I ask you now
Why you just smile
And walk away from me?

You say good-byes seem like the end
Something you hope will never be.

I heard good-byes aren't forever
I say-
And I believe that's true.

Maybe,
You say-
But I don't want
To take that chance with you.

Little Bluebird

Little bluebird in the sky
Come close to me as you fly.

Tell me all your secrets dear.
Tell me, is my lover near?

Tell me, is he on his way?
A safe return is what I pray.

Little bluebird
Oh so near,
Come close to me
Have no fear.

Tell me all your secrets dear.
Tell me, is my lover near?

My Lover

Dark eyes, Dark hair-
The scent of leather in the air

Mingled with a man's cologne
Of piney trees
And chilly sea breeze-

A scent erotic
And all his own

Strong arms
Broad shoulders
Engulfed in leather and wool

I hold on tight
Warm and sure

Snow again
No longer bright
We seek shelter
And fire light

Velvet smooth skin
Of golden bronze
Waves of love
From the beyond

Touch of fire
Intense desire

I close my eyes,
Is it a dream?
Is it false,
All I've seen?

Ecstatic feeling
As I look down,
And see your skin
Of golden brown.

Luna

I see you there, Luna,
Reflecting us light
When we close the curtains
On our day

You see us race in our minds
When the dark comes for us, and
We pray for sleep to
Forget the images
That prick our eyes with
Memories of long ago,

Haunting-

Yet, our souls reach up!
To remind us from within
To reach for the Light
Because the Light is good

And darkness is but a choice

And when you, Luna, also
Rest from reflection

We know we are not alone
For our Creator is watching over us-

And we are satisfied!

And the new morning sun is always
beautiful

A Love Like Ours

We buried him on a day
Much like today
Cold and windy with
Rain clouds in the sky

If you ask me what I was feeling
At that moment
I would say a quiet hysteria-

Because I kept wanting to laugh

We sat under the blue canopy
Our heads bowed as our pastor
Stood over the casket-
Saying words I didn't care to hear

I kept thinking of his mother's words
The evening before
During the night vigil
Faint, but audible-

"He hates dark places."

We had been speaking softly-
Telling jokes and old family stories,
It helped to ease the pain and
Quicken time

Everyone turned to her,
As she dabbed tears from her eyes
Her husband patted her back-
A feeble attempt at comfort

"He hates dark places!" she repeated-
Thinking back in time to her small child

Isn't that normal for someone to think of at a viewing?

When you see your loved one
In the open casket, but
Your mind can't escape the fact that
Soon, the lid will be closed-

Engulfing the body in darkness-

I don't know.

But on the morning of his burial
Our pastor spoke of those who have
Fallen asleep

He told us not to grieve as those who
Have no hope-

I burrowed deep into my coat
As the giggles moved up my abdomen
Making my breasts quiver-

And I continued to gaze at
The source of my amusement

It crawled at a snail's pace
Across the green turf

I assumed it was looking for the soil it
Had been disturbed from

It lingered a few feet in front of me-
Between me and the casket

Joseph's body was in there...
In that dark place-

I could see us then-

Me, at age seven,
Running for my life
As a worm or two
Were thrown my way

A regular occurrence it seemed

And Joey, age nine, laughing-

Finding it funny enough to be worth the
Reprimands from our mothers

And now, fast forward
To that cold and windy day

When I could imagine my
Handsome, loving, wild man-
Jokester, even in death-

Making a deal with the heavens
To bring this little worm to pause
Between us-

To remind me of our happy childhood

To help me understand that he is just
Sleeping-

And, yes!

I will see my husband again…

Someday-
.
.
.
I smile

I breathe

As The Dawn

As the dawn
Reached past my window,
I awoke from a horrible dream

That you walked away
With not a word to say
As you hurried fast from me

As the dawn
Reached past my window,
I awoke with a frightful start

Unwilling to accept the story
That from you I should part

Then I saw you asleep beside me
Breathing softly where you rest

I snuggled close beside you
Laid my arm across your chest

As the dawn
Reached past my window,
I'm sure I soundly fell asleep

Praying sweetly for a story
Of a love I get to keep

And in case you ever wonder-
No, I'm not leery of the dawn

For you were always with me
It was only a nightmare
That you were gone

About The Author

Nely Sanchez is the author-illustrator of the *Tallulah Spider* children's book series.

She is also the creator of several productivity planners and journals:

- *The Weekly Prep!* Planner
- *Keep the Vision:* A 90-Day Planner & Daily Goal Setting Journal
- *The Write Daily* Journal

Originally from Chicago, she now makes her home in the Desert Southwest with her husband and their four children.

Hearts Crossing is her first collection of poetry.

www.ingramcontent.com/pod-product-compliance
Lightning Source LLC
Chambersburg PA
CBHW052123110526
44592CB00013B/1723